EVERYBODY'S FRIEND

A Play

DAVID CAMPTON

SAMUEL FRENCH

LONDON

NEW YORK TORONTO SYDNEY HOLLYWOOD

CHARACTERS

Mrs Roberts
Miss Elsa Furley
Miss Daisy Loxton
Doctor (this character can be male or female)

Optional non-speaking characters

Mrs Craven
Mrs Morley
Mrs Bains
Mrs Dale
Mrs Maxby

The action takes place in two old people's flats, similar in design, and on the landing and balcony between

PRODUCTION NOTE

Miss Loxton's door need not be practical, but a panel which can be broken by Miss Furley's crutch (e.g. of cardboard or balsa-wood) would be useful. Mrs Roberts will be helped with some of her entrances if there is room to get round behind the backing.

If resources are limited the non-speaking characters need not appear. Mrs Roberts may indicate them in the direction of the audience.

EVERBODY'S FRIEND

Miss Loxton's and Miss Furley's flats are adjacent. Miss Furley's flat is austere with only one plant on the sideboard, while Miss Loxton's is filled to overflowing with pot plants. Otherwise, the rooms are a mirror image of each other, both with windows on to a small balcony thirteen floors up

In front of the flats is the landing with Miss Furley's front door on one side and Miss Loxton's on the other. Off each flat is a door leading to a kitchen

Lights up on the landing

Mrs Roberts is busy with mop and bucket. Mrs Craven hurriedly crosses the landing with the barest nod to Mrs Roberts

Mrs Roberts Cleanliness is next to you know what, Mrs Craven. How's Mr Craven? Been giving him the bran, have you? Mr Roberts always believed in bran.

By now Mrs Craven is out of sight

Huh! Always in a hurry, that one. More haste, less time to be friendly, I say. One of these days somebody is going to need help, and when they do . . .

A muffled cry comes from Miss Furley's door. Mrs Roberts listens for a second or two, then hurries over to it

Miss Furley (*off*) Help! Help!
Mrs Roberts (*with her ear to the door*) Is that you, Miss Furley?
Miss Furley (*off*) Help!
Mrs Roberts Did you say "Help"?
Miss Furley (*off*) Help!
Mrs Roberts What's the matter?
Miss Furley (*off. Slowly and louder*) My leg. I fell. I dragged myself to the door, but I can't reach the catch.
Mrs Roberts Your leg, you said?
Miss Furley (*off*) Broken.

Mrs Roberts Broken? Don't you worry. I'll dial nine-nine-nine. We'll soon have you in hospital.
Miss Furley (*off*) No!

Mrs Roberts picks up her mop and bucket and hurries off

The Lights fade and come up on Miss Furley's flat

Miss Furley is in the easy chair. The Doctor is packing

Miss Furley No. No. No. No.
Doctor My dear Miss Furley, try to see sense. You can be looked after in hospital. Here . . .
Miss Furley Save your breath, Doctor. I refuse to be moved.
Doctor You can't stay here.
Miss Furley I shall not leave.
Doctor You're . . .
Miss Furley An obstinate old woman?
Doctor I was about to say, suffering from some confusion.
Miss Furley Not to mention a broken leg. It's a disagreeable situation and I'm in some pain in spite of your sedatives, but my mind is quite clear, and made up.
Doctor I cannot take the responsibility. You should be in hospital.

Mrs Roberts enters

Mrs Roberts Can I help?
Miss Furley What are you doing here?
Mrs Roberts The front door was open. Mrs Roberts, Doctor. The one who phoned. The duty that lies nearest, you know. I've always been one for the duty that lies nearest, even when Mr Roberts was alive. What can I do now?
Miss Furley Nothing.
Mrs Roberts The ambulance is downstairs. They are good, aren't they?
Miss Furley Tell them to go away.
Mrs Roberts But you need the ambulance.
Miss Furley Allow me to be the judge of that.
Doctor You are not the doctor in this case, Miss Furley.
Miss Furley I am the patient, and I know my rights.
Doctor You could die.

Miss Furley I shall not be parted from . . . (*She breaks off, slightly confused*) I shall not . . . Leave me.

Mrs Roberts Yes. Leave us a minute, Doctor. (*She pushes the Doctor towards the door*)

Doctor What the . . .?

Mrs Roberts (*in a heavy whisper with a wink and a nod*) Just a minute.

Bemused, the Doctor goes out

Miss Furley I don't want to—talk.

Mrs Roberts (*walking to the window*) Nice place here.

Miss Furley Are you satisfied now you've seen inside?

Mrs Roberts You can see right over the railway. (*Going to Miss Furley*) You've got friends, Miss F.

Miss Furley I don't make friends.

Mrs Roberts A friend in need is worth a handful of get-well cards. We can visit you in hospital.

Miss Furley I have always lived on my own. If I have to die that way . . .

Mrs Roberts If you're worried about this flat . . .

Miss Furley I'm not . . .

Mrs Roberts (*looking round*) Leave the spit and polishing to me. Let me have the key, and I'll come in and dust. Clean the windows, too. Water the plant. (*She picks it up*)

Miss Furley (*almost beside herself*) Take your hands away from it.

Mrs Roberts (*understanding*) Ah! (*She puts the plant down*)

Miss Furley (*apologetically*) It—can't bear to be touched. I can handle it, of course. It's used to my fingers.

Mrs Roberts You couldn't take this to hospital with you.

Miss Furley I wipe the leaves regularly. It—appreciates little attentions.

Mrs Roberts You could show someone else how to wipe them.

Miss Furley I'm not leaving it.

Mrs Roberts If anything happened to you, there'd be nobody to wipe the leaves.

Miss Furley Go away. Please.

Mrs Roberts I'm not much of a one for greenery myself. I'm better with plastic. I've still got a bunch of daffodils they gave away with soap flakes years ago. But Miss Loxton now . . . You know Miss Loxton, don't you?

Miss Furley No.

Mrs Roberts Not Daisy Loxton next door? She's a wonder with pot plants. She talks to them.

Miss Furley She . . .?

Mrs Roberts "A few words of encouragement are worth all your fertilizer", she told me.

Miss Furley Miss—?

Mrs Roberts Loxton. She'd be about your age, give or take a year. You ought to have a word with her. I'll nip round and see if she's in.

Miss Furley There's no need.

Mrs Roberts A stitch in time could save a leg, Miss Furley. If Daisy Loxton were to look after your plant . . . The ambulance is still here.

Miss Furley I told the doctor . . .

Mrs Roberts I'll take it to Daisy Loxton, shall I? (*She picks up the plant*) I can come out to the hospital. Any time you like. I'll let you know how it's getting on. You don't have to worry about a thing. All right, Doctor, you can come in now.

Mrs Roberts goes into the kitchen

The Doctor enters, glaring back

Doctor Perhaps a tranquillizer . . . Not for you, Miss Furley. For me after two minutes with that woman . . . Don't you worry. We'll soon have you in plaster.

The Lights fade and come up on Miss Loxton's flat

Mrs Roberts enters with Miss Loxton, who carries the plant

Mrs Roberts (*laughing*) Of course we ought not to laugh with the poor dear done up in plaster. Shock takes people different ways. The day after we buried Mr Roberts I sat through *The Sound of Music* three times running.

Miss Loxton Tell her I give him a drop of cold tea every morning.

Mrs Roberts Cold tea? (*She laughs*) With milk and sugar?

Miss Loxton You don't know much about plants, Mrs Roberts. I make a good strong pot first thing in the morning. Nothing like a real dark cup for waking you up. When the pot's near empty I fill her up with cold water. That's for my dears. You

tell your Miss Furley I treat him no better and no worse than
my other dears.

Mrs Roberts Pull the other one, Daisy Loxton. It's got bells on.

Miss Loxton I'm afraid you don't know much about anything,
Mrs Roberts. I don't have favourites. 'Tisn't fair when they're
all doing their best. That's the trouble with this world. Them as
has has their hases added to. Them as hasn't are pushed into
corners and forgot. Well, it's not like that here. I love them all.
Don't I, my lovelies?

Mrs Roberts Is that what I'm supposed to tell Miss F.?

Miss Loxton Tell her, weak tea and affection.

Mrs Roberts Weak tea.

Miss Loxton And affection.

Mrs Roberts shrugs her shoulders and goes out

Miss Loxton Especially affection.

*The Lights fade and come up on the landing and Miss Furley's flat
Miss Furley enters her living-room supported by crutches, and
followed by Mrs Roberts*

Miss Furley No, no. Don't support me. I may be assisted by
crutches but I can manipulate them myself.

Mrs Roberts I'll keep popping in to make sure you're all right.

Miss Furley (*lowering herself into her easy chair*) Mrs Roberts—I
—I am grateful for all you have done. I realize that I should
have been in a sorry plight if you had not answered my call for
help. But I shall not need—constant attendance. (*Looking
wildly around*) Where is it?

Mrs Roberts I warned you to take it easy.

Miss Furley Where—is—it?

Mrs Roberts At your age you don't mend as fast as a youngster.

Miss Furley What have you done with it?

Mrs Roberts Don't jump off the deep end. You never know
where you may land. (*She laughs*)

Miss Furley (*struggling to get out of the chair*) You lied, didn't
you? Anything to keep her calm. That was the official attitude.
How did you dispose of the remains? Did you bury them?
Burn them? Throw them out with the potato parings? What
have you done with the pot?

Miss Loxton crosses the landing with the plant, shielded by a piece of paper. She rings at Miss Furley's door

Mrs Roberts I expect that's Daisy Loxton now. Bringing it back.
Miss Furley The pot?
Mrs Roberts The plant. You're going to be surprised.

Mrs Roberts leaves the living-room

Miss Furley waits impatiently

A few seconds later the front door is opened and Miss Loxton goes in

Mrs Roberts (*off*) Oh, yes. Take it off.

Miss Furley struggles to turn round in her chair, which has its back to the door, but gives up

Miss Loxton enters the living-room in front of Mrs Roberts. She has taken the protecting paper from the plant, revealing a spike of bright red flowers sticking up in the middle. She holds it out to Miss Furley

Miss Furley does not take it

Miss Furley It—flowered!
Miss Loxton It flowered.
Miss Furley It never flowered before.
Mrs Roberts Put it down while I get tea.
Miss Furley It flowered while I was away.

Miss Loxton takes the plant to the sideboard and puts it down

Miss Loxton Handsome, isn't it? A great red spike.
Miss Furley I didn't even know it was supposed to flower.
Miss Loxton Most of 'em do if they're treated properly.
Miss Furley Implying that I failed?
Miss Loxton They have their fads and foibles like the rest of us.
Miss Furley Cold tea?
Mrs Roberts Hot and sweet. Won't be long.

Mrs Roberts goes into the kitchen

Miss Loxton I give them all cold tea. I couldn't leave one out, could I? Just because he was a stranger. That would have been discrimination, my dear. I don't have favourites, and I try not to discriminate.

Miss Furley Are you sure this is my plant?

Miss Loxton Can you doubt it? When it's so pleased to see you.

Miss Furley Is it?

Miss Loxton He flowered.

Miss Furley My plant had no red appendages.

Miss Loxton They like encouragement. That doesn't sound like encouragement.

Miss Furley Did you encourage it to assume this garish display?

Miss Loxton I wonder—did you encourage enough?

Miss Furley I attended to its needs.

Miss Loxton They respond to that little extra. After all human beings do, so why not plants?

Miss Furley I have never been party to bribery, either towards plants or humans. I pay for what I receive, and expect to receive what I pay for. I have no truck with trading stamps or bargain offers. A bribe demeans the one who offers and the one who accepts.

Miss Loxton My father said I had green fingers.

Miss Furley Unpleasant expression. (*She decides to change the subject*) You must tell me what I owe you.

Miss Loxton Owe?

Miss Furley For taking care of . . .

Miss Loxton It was a pleasure.

Miss Furley The pleasure was incidental. I must owe you something. I believe in discharging my debts.

Miss Loxton Well, if you insist . . .

Miss Furley How much?

Miss Loxton Just let me come in and have a look at him from time to time.

Miss Furley At—him?

Miss Loxton I can't think of a better payment.

Miss Furley I didn't expect . . .

Miss Loxton I'd not like to think I'd seen the last. After being so close.

Miss Furley If—if you insist. I can hardly refuse. From time to time.

Miss Loxton And don't you go worrying about that flower, my dear. He'll be back to normal in a couple of weeks, exactly as you always knew him.

Miss Furley Not exactly. There have been changes. We must adjust to them. Now, if you don't mind . . . I should like to be alone. The day has been tiring, and . . .

Mrs Roberts appears in the doorway

Mrs Roberts Kettle's boiling.
Miss Furley Alone, Mrs Roberts.
Mrs Roberts But you can't stand at the sink with one leg.
Miss Furley Alone, alone, alone, alone.
Miss Loxton Very well, my dear. (*She goes to Mrs Roberts*)
Mrs Roberts But . . .
Miss Loxton This way. (*She urges Mrs Roberts out*)

Miss Furley struggles from her chair and crosses to the sideboard. She glares at the plant

Miss Furley Well? What more is there to say? I detest disloyalty. Cupboard love. Boot-licking. Fawning. And for what? Cold tea! She talks to them, does she? As she talked to you. Coaxing in that West Country croon of hers. Flattery. And you soaked it all in like the—the cold tea. I can't flatter. A fatal defect, I suppose. Men expect it. If you weren't happy with me, why didn't you die like the rest? If you didn't die with me, why did you flower for her? She talked to you, did she? Well, I am talking now. And I am telling you the truth. Your conduct was despicable. Despicable, understand? We shall not refer to the incident again. It was a lapse that must be forgiven. But we must not be reminded. (*She takes a large pair of scissors from the sideboard*) I must cut that flower. I must cut it out. Right out.

As she cuts the flower Miss Loxton appears in the kitchen doorway, catching her with the flower in one hand and the scissors in the other

Miss Loxton You cut it off, my dear?
Miss Furley It was necessary.
Miss Loxton Necessary?
Miss Furley This flower was not necessary. We had been together for five years. Mere foliage was sufficient. Why should there

have been a flower after five years? (*She returns to her easy chair, and sits*)

Miss Loxton They flower when they must. He looks different without . . .

Miss Furley As I intended.

Miss Loxton Depressed.

Miss Furley Normal.

Miss Loxton Unhappy.

Miss Furley Plants are neither happy nor unhappy. They exist.

Miss Loxton For our pleasure. We ought to consider their feelings.

Miss Furley They exist. That is all. A vegetable with feelings? Let us keep a sense of proportion.

Miss Loxton I can tell.

Miss Furley With your plants. This one happens to be mine.

Miss Loxton Pity you had to cut it off. He might have seeded.

Miss Furley Not this plant.

Miss Loxton You'll be taking cuttings, then?

Miss Furley Cuttings?

Miss Loxton Propagation, my dear.

Miss Furley There will be no propagation here.

Miss Loxton But how else will you get the others, my dear?

Miss Furley This plant is unique. It has always been unique. It will remain unique.

Miss Loxton But if he should die?

Miss Furley Die?

Miss Loxton Without seedlings or cuttings, where will you be?

Miss Furley Alone. I can face facts. Have you seen enough?

Miss Loxton Too much, maybe.

Miss Furley Miss Loxton . . .

Miss Loxton Daisy, my dear.

Miss Furley Please don't be offended at what I am about to say . . .

Miss Loxton I don't offend easy.

Miss Furley I think you may have taken too much interest in this particular plant.

Miss Loxton 'Tis hard not to feel a tug at parting. I had him all those weeks.

Miss Furley The plant was merely fostered with you. Nothing permanent was intended.

Miss Loxton Of course not. He's yours.

Miss Furley Why must you keep calling it "he"?

Miss Loxton Because he is a he. After what happened who could deny that? As plain a he as ever I watered.

Miss Furley It—belongs here.

Miss Loxton That's right, my dear. He belongs where he'll be loved.

Miss Furley Loved?

Miss Loxton And cared for.

Miss Furley I don't know what you mean by loved.

Miss Loxton Oh, it doesn't matter what word you use, my dear. It's the feeling that counts . . . I must be going. No, keep that leg rested. Old bones don't knit easy. I remember the trouble I had with Father. Lost his leg at seventy, and still went on another nine years. I'll be in again to see how my Joey's faring.

Miss Furley Joey!

Miss Loxton And not mine, of course. Only for a week or so. Yours really. I'll be round again in a day or so.

Miss Furley I'd rather you didn't.

Miss Loxton You don't . . .?

Miss Furley Was that too blunt? I'm sorry. But at least there is no room for misunderstandings.

Miss Loxton Why?

Miss Furley Say that it is best for both of us.

Miss Loxton There was a promise.

Miss Furley And this is poor thanks for your kindness. I am ashamed to sound so churlish, but my mind is made up. It's for the best. It really is.

Miss Loxton It's him, isn't it? Where's the harm in just looking?

Miss Furley Because temptation begins with just looking.

Miss Loxton What must you think of me?

Miss Furley We are all subject to temptation, Miss Loxton. Believe me I'm grateful for . . .

Miss Loxton I'd have done it for anybody. I've a great respect for plants, you see. In fact the more I see of people, the more respect I have for plants.

Miss Loxton goes out

Miss Furley Oh, people! People. Why must they intrude? They only have to speak to spoil . . . Joey! She called you Joey! When your name is George Frederick.

The Lights fade and come up on Miss Furley's living-room. Miss Furley is in the easy chair, taking groceries from a bag and handing them to Mrs Roberts

Mrs Roberts Butter. Cheese. Tea.
Miss Furley This isn't my usual tea.
Mrs Roberts It's the tea that Daisy Loxton has.
Miss Furley I prefer my own brand.
Mrs Roberts Ah, but what about that one on the sideboard?

(*She goes to the sideboard and looks at the plant*)

Miss Furley We are back to a diet of rain-water. I collect it on the balcony. (*She rummages in the bag*) I can't see any dried peas.
Mrs Roberts Oh, pudding-head me. I'll nip in again tomorrow. You know, looking at it close . . . (*She turns the pot round. A number of leaves are hanging limply*)
Miss Furley We are unpacking my groceries, Mrs Roberts.
Mrs Roberts Are the leaves supposed to dangle like that?
Miss Furley There aren't any butter beans, either.
Mrs Roberts They hadn't got any so I brought haricot. If you ask me, it's looking poorly.
Miss Furley In future I'll go down to the shops myself.

Mrs Roberts goes back to Miss Furley and replaces the groceries in the bag

Mrs Roberts Think nothing of it. According to Daisy Loxton some plants need a lot of water, and some don't like any.
Miss Furley I know his preferences by now.
Mrs Roberts I don't like the look of those leaves hanging down.
Miss Furley There are certain times of year . . .
Mrs Roberts Oh, they've drooped before, have they? I'll take the bag into the kitchen. Daisy Loxton always asks about it most particular. You don't mind if I tell her how it's getting on?

Mrs Roberts goes into the kitchen with the bag

Miss Furley You will. Whatever my wishes, I've no doubt you will.
Mrs Roberts (*off*) Ta-ta.

Miss Furley gets up and goes to the plant

Miss Furley You're wilting. Pull yourself together. You've never wilted before. You didn't even wilt when you left me for her. Why then should you wilt when you leave her for me? Sulking? Why should you sulk? Because I don't talk to you as she talked to you? There's more than one sort of person in this world, just as there is more than one sort of plant. If I don't croon, it's not because I feel any the less. There are certain emotions that one cannot express even to oneself. Or are you ill? Ill! You must not be ill. There are certain necessities one cannot own, even to oneself. You must recover. A little more rain-water? Very well, then. Cold tea.

Miss Furley takes the plant into the kitchen

The Lights fade and come up on Miss Loxton's flat

Mrs Roberts enters with Miss Loxton

Mrs Roberts But you don't need me to tell you.
Miss Loxton No dear, you don't need to tell me.
Mrs Roberts That plant's . . .
Miss Loxton Dying, dear.
Mrs Roberts Only sick as yet.
Miss Loxton I know only two ends to sickness. Either he gets better or . . . What if he's not cured?
Mrs Roberts She does her best, I'm sure.
Miss Loxton She's no feeling for him.
Mrs Roberts You're wrong there. One look at those brown leaves and she reaches for the aspirin bottle.
Miss Loxton She's no instinct. Such people should not be allowed near a plant. I'll tell you this, my dear. If he stays next door with her, the last word's been said.
Mrs Roberts Hope springs, I always say.
Miss Loxton Hope's a poor medicine. If only he were to stay over here with me—just for a few weeks, just to give him the chance to gather his resources. She went into hospital, didn't she? Would she deny him the same advantages?
Mrs Roberts You have a way of putting things. I'll tell her that right now.

Mrs Roberts exits

Miss Loxton She won't listen, my dear. She won't listen.

Miss Loxton follows Mrs Roberts

The Lights fade and come up on Miss Furley's living-room

Miss Furley enters from the kitchen carrying a very bedraggled plant which she puts on the sideboard

Miss Furley (*talking back to the kitchen*) I am not listening. You have been plotting with her. You carry her tales and tarra-diddles.

Mrs Roberts enters from the kitchen with a teapot

Mrs Roberts I do what I can for everybody. Everybody's friend, that's me.
Miss Furley She has one ambition: to possess him.
Mrs Roberts (*moving to the sideboard*) She wants him to get better. If you were to let me take it to her . . .
Miss Furley (*agitated*) If you touch that pot, I shall strike you.
Mrs Roberts There's no need to wave your crutch at me, Miss F.
Miss Furley I have a right to defend my property. There are thieves at my very door.
Mrs Roberts Daisy Loxton isn't.
Miss Furley She has coveted him since she first saw him. That is a sin.
Mrs Roberts Strong language, Miss F.
Miss Furley Thou shalt not covet thy neighbour's house, nor his wife, nor his ox, nor his ass, nor anything that is thy neighbour's; and that includes his potted plant. As you are so free with Miss Loxton, warn her that I shall protect my own.
Mrs Roberts It won't be your own much longer if leaves fall off at that rate.

She realizes that she is gesturing with the teapot and takes it back into the kitchen

Miss Furley I cradled him. I nursed him. If necessary I shall bury him. I and no other. If Miss Loxton tries to come between us . . . A nod is as good as a wink, as you must have said.

Miss Furley exits

The Lights fade and come up on Miss Loxton's flat

*Miss Loxton enters followed by Mrs Roberts carrying a different
teapot*

Miss Loxton She'll let him die sooner than let him go.

Mrs Roberts Then there'll be an end. The sooner the better. You
wouldn't want the poor thing to linger. Though I don't suppose
vegetables feel the way we do.

Miss Loxton It must not happen.

Mrs Roberts What must be must be prepared for, that's what I
always say. I keep trying to persuade Mr Craven to take out a
policy, if only to cover the funeral expenses, but he doesn't see
things my way. Did you know that young Mr Green in twenty-
seven sells insurance? Very convenient.

Miss Loxton He must be saved.

Mrs Roberts It's quite a respectable job, as long as you don't
push your policies too hard. Or do you mean Mr Brown? He's
the one on probation for breaking and entering.

Miss Loxton He must be saved from her.

Mrs Roberts I don't know. He never mentioned a her.

Miss Loxton Her next door. If she won't give him up, other ways
must be found. Is it possible, do you think, to climb from this
balcony to the other?

Mrs Roberts It's the thirteenth floor. You're an active woman for
your age, Daisy, but I can't see you swinging over balconies.
(*She guffaws*)

Miss Loxton How did Mr What'shisname do it? What tools did
he use?

Mrs Roberts That depends on who you mean and what he was
doing.

Miss Loxton He broke and entered.

Mrs Roberts He wants to forget all that. He's paid his debt to
society. At least, being on parole, he's owing it. He told me so.

Miss Loxton A way in must be found.

Mrs Roberts I always knock at the door myself.

Miss Loxton That plant, my dear, is dying of a broken heart.

Mrs Roberts If you don't watch yourself, Daisy, you're going to
run right off the rails.

Miss Loxton If necessary, I'll fetch him myself.

Mrs Roberts It's against the law. You ask Mr Brown.
Miss Loxton I shall. Would he do it for me if I paid enough?
  After all, he's a professional.
Mrs Roberts You're not to tempt Mr Brown, Daisy. He's trying
  to go straight. I wouldn't have him put inside again for the
  whole of the botanical gardens, let alone . . .
Miss Loxton There's so little time.
Mrs Roberts You're smothered in plants here. Spider plants and
  coleus. What's one more or less.
Miss Loxton I'd part with them all for that one. He's dying for
  me.
Mrs Roberts He's not dying for anybody. He's just dying.
Miss Loxton One never died for me before.
Mrs Roberts Daisy, you're not yourself this afternoon. You used
  to be the voice of common-sense. "Compost", you used to say,
  or "A pinch of Glauber salts". Never anything like burglary.
Miss Loxton If she won't give him up, he must be taken.
Mrs Roberts It's her plant. She's every right to do what she likes
  with it.
Miss Loxton Nobody has the right to murder.
Mrs Roberts It's only half a dozen spotty leaves.
Miss Loxton Down to half a dozen now! You didn't tell me that.
Mrs Roberts Six. Eight. Ten. Twelve. What does it matter?
Miss Loxton There's less time than I thought. It must be today.
  Tomorrow at the latest.
Mrs Roberts I'm ashamed of you, Daisy, talking of robbing
  friends.
Miss Loxton Nobody can stop me.
Mrs Roberts I can, Daisy.
Miss Loxton You can't hold me back.
Mrs Roberts I can warn her.
Miss Loxton You wouldn't!
Mrs Roberts I'll put her on her guard.
Miss Loxton When will you learn to keep out of other people's
  business?
Mrs Roberts Me?
Miss Loxton Probing and prompting and prying. Look after
  your own interests and interfere less with mine.
Mrs Roberts I like that. You'd never have known what was
  happening next door if it hadn't been for me.

Miss Loxton I'd have slept easy, not knowing. I wouldn't have needed to hurt her or put myself in danger.

Mrs Roberts You don't have to.

Miss Loxton (*suddenly conciliatory*) Of course not, my dear. I'm sorry words were spoken. Just forget the subject was ever raised. (*She takes the teapot from Mrs Roberts*) Why, the tea's quite cold. I'll put the kettle on again.

Miss Loxton takes the teapot into the kitchen

Mrs Roberts I'll have to tell her. It's only fair. She has a right.

Miss Loxton (*off*) She won't thank you, my dear.

The Lights fade and come up on both flats

Miss Loxton comes from her kitchen with an ironing-board which she takes out on to the balcony, and disappears from sight. Shortly afterwards she appears on Miss Furley's balcony. She busies herself with the lock on the window. The window opens and she steps into Miss Furley's living-room. She takes the plant out via the balcony, appearing shortly afterwards at her own window

Miss Furley and Mrs Roberts cross the landing to Miss Furley's flat and go in

Miss Loxton scuttles into her kitchen with the plant and the ironing-board

As soon as Miss Furley enters her living-room she notices the empty sideboard

Miss Furley Where is he?

Mrs Roberts (*off*) Who?

Miss Furley (*hobbling into the room*) Him.

Mrs Roberts appears in the doorway

Mrs Roberts What?

Miss Furley Gone.

Mrs Roberts Where?

Miss Furley Gone.

Mrs Roberts I'll have a look around. Seek and ye shall remember where you put it.

Miss Furley Gone. (*She sinks into the easy chair*)
Mrs Roberts Chin up. Cheer up. That's what I used to say to
  Mr Roberts.

Mrs Roberts goes into the kitchen

Miss Furley Gone.
Mrs Roberts (*off*) I can't see it in here.
Miss Furley Gone.
Mrs Roberts (*off*) Nor in the bedroom.
Miss Furley Gone.

Mrs Roberts returns

Mrs Roberts I can't see it anywhere. It's not in the kitchen; it's
  not in the bedroom; it's not in the bathroom.
Miss Furley Gone.
Mrs Roberts That's the trouble with these old people's flats, there
  isn't room to lose anything.
Miss Furley Gone.
Mrs Roberts Now let's put our thinking caps on. When did you
  see it last?
Miss Furley He was there when I left the flat. There. I waved and
  one leaf stirred feebly.
Mrs Roberts It's not there now.
Miss Furley Gone. I must call the police.
Mrs Roberts What can the police do?
Miss Furley They can arrest that fiend next door.
Mrs Roberts I don't think they would.
Miss Furley Is she to be allowed to maraud unrestrained? Are
  our nearest and dearest to be spirited away while she goes free?
  She must be put away. Call them. Now. I have been robbed.
  The law is the law. Thou shalt not steal.
Mrs Roberts The police are going to ask questions that are hard
  to answer. Can you prove that you ever had a plant on the
  sideboard? They're going to ask.
Miss Furley The Loxton woman took him from there.
Mrs Roberts Daisy Loxton isn't going to confess just like that.
Miss Furley Am I denied justice?
Mrs Roberts Ask yourself, are Scotland Yard likely to investigate
  a dead plant?
Miss Furley He's not dead.

Mrs Roberts It could well be by the time they found it.
Miss Furley Very well, then. I shall take the law into my own
hands.

Miss Furley goes into the kitchen, followed by Mrs Roberts

The Lights fade and come up on Miss Loxton's flat

*Miss Loxton enters clutching the plant which she takes to the
balcony*

Miss Loxton Out on the balcony to catch the sun and air, my
dear. The air is clean and fresh up here. Thirteen floors up.
You'll grow up fine and strong. That's the way it was meant to
be.

The Lights fade and come up on the landing

*Miss Furley comes from her front door, followed by Mrs Roberts.
They cross to Miss Loxton's front door*

Mrs Roberts Tell you what, get another plant, eh? A cyclamen
or a chrysanthemum. The shops are full of them. And if
anything goes wrong, you can always get another.
Miss Furley (*shouting*) I am roused! (*She beats on Miss Loxton's
door*) Open this door.
Mrs Roberts This isn't the way to go about it.
Miss Furley Bitch!
Mrs Roberts Miss Furley!
Miss Furley Adulterous thief.
Mrs Roberts You don't use such words.
Miss Furley Lecherous cat.
Mrs Roberts You're not supposed to know what they mean.
Miss Furley Open up.
Mrs Roberts Let's try to talk it over quietly.
Miss Furley Bring him back.

A small crowd begins to gather

Mrs Roberts Doors are opening all over the landing. Afternoon,
Mrs Morley. Just a friendly call.
Miss Furley I know you have him in there—you—you concubine.
Mrs Roberts Don't say anything you'll be sorry for.

Miss Furley Open. Open. Open.
Mrs Roberts She won't you know. Be honest. Would you?
Miss Furley Libertine.
Mrs Roberts Be careful. If it's not true, she could have you for slander. Hello, Mrs Bains. No need to get upset. My friend's not quite herself just now.
Miss Furley Trollop.
Mrs Roberts People are coming upstairs, Miss F.
Miss Furley Jezebel. You can hear me, can't you?
Mrs Roberts They can hear you three floors down.
Miss Furley If you don't open this door, I'll break it down. (*She hits the door with her crutch*)
Mrs Roberts Not with your crutch, dear. You're going to need it.
Miss Furley And when I've broken the door . . .
Mrs Roberts At least don't hold on to me while you do it.
Miss Furley I'll break your damned neck. (*She hits the door again*)
Mrs Roberts I'm not really an accessory, Mrs Dale, but if I move away, she'll fall down.
Miss Furley Say your prayers. (*She hits the door*)
Mrs Roberts These doors won't stand it.
Miss Furley Whore!
Mrs Roberts Mr Dalby put his foot right through, and he was only drunk.
Miss Furley Rapist. (*She hits the door*)
Mrs Roberts People are staring. Just a slight disappointment, Mrs Maxby. They're really the best of friends.

Miss Furley hits the door repeatedly with her crutch

Miss Furley There. There. There. There.

The sound of distant police sirens grows louder

Mrs Roberts Here come the police. Come away.

The Lights fade as the sound of the sirens grows louder. The sirens fade and the Lights come up on Miss Furley's flat

   Miss Furley enters with Mrs Roberts

Mrs Roberts You mustn't give way, Miss F. People come up in front of the magistrates every day. After all they only gave you a conditional discharge. My goodness, there's many serving six months who'd have been glad of a conditional discharge. That's the sort of silver lining you've got to look for.

Miss Furley sinks dejectedly into the easy chair

Miss Furley (*in a flat voice*) Was it always meant to be like this?
Mrs Roberts And you're going to be friends with Daisy Loxton.
Miss Furley You stretch out your hand for something to love, and it withers at a touch.
Mrs Roberts You are going to put an end to this silly quarrel. The pair of you losing weight, losing colour, losing sleep. I am going to do something about it, I said.
Miss Furley You mustn't, Mrs Roberts.
Mrs Roberts I won't be satisfied until I've seen you shake hands.
Miss Furley I ought to warn you, Mrs Roberts.
Mrs Roberts I know what has to be done.
Miss Furley A tragedy is a heavy piece of machinery, dangerous to get in the way of. When it starts to move it could run you over.
Mrs Roberts You're coming with me to Daisy Loxton again.
Miss Furley The machinery started to move some time ago.
Mrs Roberts Now.
Miss Furley No.
Mrs Roberts I won't budge from this spot till you agree.
Miss Furley You don't know much about people, Mrs Roberts. Perhaps you watch too much television. You think life goes on behind an oblong screen, that what happens can't touch you.
Mrs Roberts After all I've done for everybody.
Miss Furley Go home, Mrs Roberts.
Mrs Roberts Not until I've done what I set out to do.
Miss Furley If I wish to loathe Miss Loxton, that is my affair. If I am denied love, at least I can hate.
Mrs Roberts Not while I'm around. Are you coming?
Miss Furley You are making a mistake.
Mrs Roberts You'll see the plant again.
Miss Furley See . . . ?
Mrs Roberts Didn't think of that, did you? Yes, you'll have to see the plant. Now do come along.
Miss Furley You leave me no option.
Mrs Roberts At last.
Miss Furley One moment. There is something in the kitchen.

Mrs Roberts I'll get it for you.
Miss Furley I would rather—I must—myself. I'll not detain you long. Then we shall be ready for . . .

She goes into the kitchen. Her last remarks come from there. Mrs Roberts goes after her

The Lights fade and come up on Miss Loxton's flat

Miss Loxton comes in talking to Miss Furley and Mrs Roberts behind her

Miss Loxton Fresh and green with lusty shoots. I won't part with him. Not if I were killed my dear. I may die with him, but I won't part with him.

Miss Furley and Mrs Roberts follow Miss Loxton

Mrs Roberts There!
Miss Furley (*cold and remote*) Miss Loxton.
Mrs Roberts (*triumphantly*) That's a beginning, isn't it? Well begun is better than not starting. That's what I say.
Miss Furley What do you say, Miss Loxton?
Miss Loxton I'm not saying anything, dear.
Miss Furley Not even "sorry"?
Miss Loxton You wouldn't have me tell an untruth, would you, dear?
Miss Furley I'd despise you if you did. It would demean him to be hidden behind a lie.
Miss Loxton I'm not admitting anything, either.
Miss Furley It's not necessary. I know what you must feel. I know what I should have done in your case. I know what I must do in mine.
Mrs Roberts That's better. Now shake hands. Go on. Shake hands.
Miss Loxton I will if she will.
Miss Furley I'm afraid I can't.
Mrs Roberts Force yourself.
Miss Furley If I shake hands the knife will slip from my sleeve.
Miss Loxton The knife?
Miss Furley This one. (*She produces a kitchen knife from her sleeve*)

Miss Loxton I told you she wanted to murder me.
Miss Furley It will be a *crime passionnel*.
Mrs Roberts Put that knife down. All these threatenings and slaughter over an old . . .
Miss Furley Where is he?
Miss Loxton I'll show you, my dear.

Miss Loxton fetches the plant from the balcony. The brown leaves have gone, and in their place are three green leaves

Miss Furley Treachery! (*She makes for Miss Loxton, but is restrained by Mrs Roberts*)
Mrs Roberts No, you don't. I'll take charge of that knife.
Miss Furley You're hurting my wrist.
Mrs Roberts Give it up.
Miss Furley You know I can only use one arm without falling down. Oh.
Mrs Roberts (*taking the knife*) Thank you. And if you don't mind, Daisy, I'll take that pot as well. (*She takes it from Miss Loxton, and sticks the knife in the pot*)
Miss Loxton What do you want with it?
Mrs Roberts When I was little, and quarrelled with my brother over a toy, my mother would take it from both of us. "If you can't agree over it," she would say, "neither of you shall have it." You'll thank me one of these days. But you've seen the last of this. (*She throws the pot over the balcony*)

Miss Loxton screams

Miss Furley Over the balcony.
Miss Loxton Thirteen floors.
Miss Furley Without a lift.
Miss Loxton 'Twill be nothing but a green smudge on the paving down there.
Miss Furley Thirteen floors.
Miss Loxton Unless he hit somebody. Then there'll be a red smudge on the paving.
Mrs Roberts Oh! I hope you realize now what your wicked tantrums lead to. If that pot hit anybody, it will be your fault.
Miss Furley You don't think ahead, Mrs Roberts.
Miss Loxton Better look down, my dear.
Miss Furley Better find out.

Mrs Roberts I'm just going to. What can't be cured has to be explained away. (*She looks over the balcony*) There are dots of people running around, and specks of people looking up here. If they're either running or looking, they can't be hurt. I can't see any smudge on the pavement. Not even where the pot landed. Somebody's waving. Either waving or shaking a fist.

Miss Furley and Miss Loxton look at each other, then silently come up behind Mrs Roberts

Mrs Roberts (*shouting*) It was an accident. I don't think they heard me. They're a long way down. (*Shouting*) It—was . . .

Miss Furley and Miss Loxton bend down and grasp Mrs Roberts' legs

Mrs Roberts Miss Loxton. Miss Furley. Stop it this minute. You could . . . I could . . . That's what you're trying to do! (*Shouting*) Help! They're tipping me over. Help! You down there. Help! Whooah! Oh. Oh. Oooooooh.

Mrs Roberts' cry fades away as she goes over the balcony

Miss Loxton Thirteen floors.
Miss Furley Without a lift. Don't look.
Miss Loxton It's better not to, dear.
Miss Furley Nothing could survive that fall.
Miss Loxton It was an accident, dear.
Miss Furley It was murder.
Miss Loxton 'Twould be a kindness to say it was an accident, my dear.
Miss Furley Very well. We'll tell the police it was an accident.
Miss Loxton The police?
Miss Furley They'll want to know.
Miss Loxton 'Twill only be a little white lie, my dear. I'll tell it if you like.
Miss Furley I shall wear black from now on.
Miss Loxton You have some lovely ideas, my dear. I'll wear black, too.
Miss Furley Friendship demands. I wonder if you'd mind—if I came back here from time to time. To revisit the spot.
Miss Loxton Come as often as you like, my dear. 'Twill be company. I'm thinking the two of us will be in need of company now.

Miss Furley You're very good, Miss Loxton.
Miss Loxton Call me Daisy.
Miss Furley My name's—Elsa.
Miss Loxton You're white and shaking.
Miss Furley I'm only just beginning to realize fully . . .
Miss Loxton Take my hand.
Miss Furley Thank you. Thirteen floors. A tragedy.
Miss Loxton Cut off so young.
Miss Furley Three new leaves.
Miss Loxton And more beginning.
Miss Furley We'll mourn him together.

The Lights fade as—

the CURTAIN *falls*

FURNITURE AND PROPERTY LIST

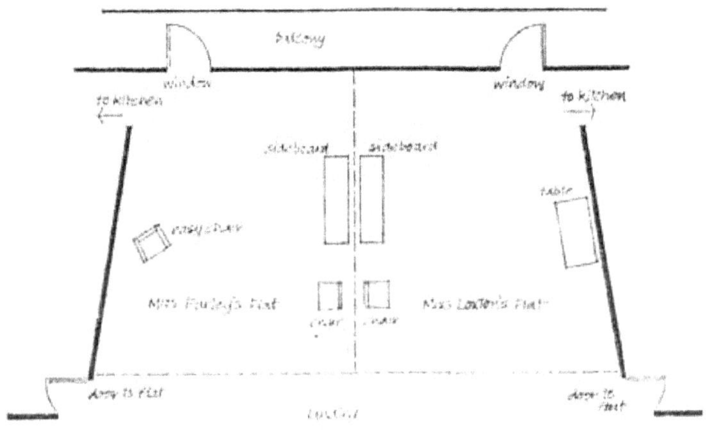

On stage: Sideboard. *On it:* green pot plant, changed to dying plant
(**Miss Furley's flat**); large number of plants (**Miss Loxton's
flat**). *In it:* large pair of scissors (**Miss Furley's flat**)
1 easy chair
2 ordinary chairs

Off stage: mop and bucket (**Mrs Roberts**)
crutches (**Miss Furley**)
plant with red flower (**Mrs Roberts**)
bag of groceries (**Mrs Roberts**)
2 different teapots (**Mrs Roberts**)
ironing-board (**Miss Loxton**)
kitchen knife (**Miss Furley**)
plant with three green leaves (**Miss Loxton**)

LIGHTING PLOT

To open: Lights up on landing

Cue 1   **Mrs Roberts** exits with mop and bucket   (Page 2)
Fade Lights, come up on Miss Furley's flat

Cue 2   **Doctor:** ". . . have you in plaster."   (Page 4)
Fade Lights, come up on Miss Loxton's flat

Cue 3   **Miss Loxton:** "Especially affection."   (Page 5)
*Fade Lights, come up on the landing and Miss
Furley's flat*

Cue 4   **Miss Furley:** ". . . your name is George Frederick." (Page 11)
Fade Lights, come up on Miss Furley's living-room

Cue 5   **Miss Furley** exits to kitchen with plant   (Page 12)
Fade Lights, come up on Miss Loxton's flat

Cue 6   **Mrs Roberts** exits followed by **Miss Loxton**   (Page 13)
Fade Lights, come up on Miss Furley's living-room

Cue 7   **Miss Furley** exits   (Page 14)
Fade Lights, come up on Miss Loxton's flat

Cue 8   **Miss Loxton:** "She won't thank you, my dear."   (Page 16)
Fade Lights, come up on both flats

Cue 9   **Miss Furley** goes into kitchen, followed by **Mrs
Roberts**   (Page 18)
Fade Lights, come up on Miss Loxton's flat

Cue 10   **Miss Loxton:** ". . . way it was meant to be."   (Page 18)
Fade Lights, come up on the landing

Cue 11   **Mrs Roberts:** "Come away."   (Page 19)
Fade Lights, come up on Miss Furley's flat

Cue 12   **Miss Furley** exits to kitchen followed by **Mrs
Roberts**   (Page 21)
Fade Lights, come up on Miss Loxton's flat

Cue 13   **Miss Furley:** "We'll mourn him together."   (Page 24)
Fade Lights to Black-out

EFFECTS PLOT

<table>
<tr><td>Cue 1</td><td>Miss Furley: "There. There. There. There."</td><td>(Page 19)</td></tr>
<tr><td></td><td colspan="2">Police sirens grow louder, fade as Lights come up on
Miss Furley's flat</td></tr>
</table>